Naming the Tree

Simon Richey

Oversteps Books

First published in 2014 by   Oversteps Books Ltd
                                 6 Halwell House
                                 South Pool
                                 Nr Kingsbridge
                                 Devon
                                 TQ7 2RX
                                 UK

www.overstepsbooks.com

Copyright © 2014 Simon Richey
ISBN 978-1-906856-46-5

All rights reserved. No part of this book may be reproduced, stored in a retrieval system, or transmitted in any form, or by any means, electronic, mechanical, photocopying, recording or otherwise, or translated into any language, without prior written permission from Oversteps Books, except by a reviewer who may quote brief passages in a review.

The right of Simon Richey to be identified as the author of this work has been asserted by him in accordance with the Copyright, Designs and Patents Act 1988.

Printed in Great Britain by imprint digital, Devon

for Anna and Peter

Acknowledgements:

Some of these poems have been published in Acumen, Magma, Poetry London, Poetry Review, Tears in the Fence, the 3rd Ware Poetry Competition Anthology and Weyfarers.

With particular thanks to Stephen Boyce and Peter Richey.

Contents

The Word	1
The Stone	2
A History of the Tongue	3
Silences	4
The Moment	6
Considering Fire	7
Visiting Birds	11
Naming the Tree	12
The Making of Nests	16
The Mistake	17
The Darkness	18
Before	21
The Bell	22
The First Bird	23
The Naming of Days	24
The Wall	26
Dead	27
Crossings	28
Something Had Been Done	31
Days	32
Rain	34
Not	36
Late January	38
One	39
Birds	40
Asides	42
Monday	43
The Fact	46
Singing the Blackbird	47
The Book	48

The Word

There was a day, there was a moment
when the word for it was spoken for the last time.

Somewhere it was uttered
and then never repeated.

And because there was no word anymore, no sound in which
its meaning could be carried,

the meaning had nowhere to go.
And so the meaning itself started to wither

because it could no longer hear itself,
because it no longer had a presence in the world.

The Stone

i

It is mottled black, the shape of an elongated egg. Lifting it from the beach that morning, throwing it lightly in the air, my open hand was the door, the warm flap through which it entered our world.
Now it sits here on the polished table, beyond the influence of the sea, the weather, beyond change. To change it now I would need to drop it, or to open it with a hammer.

ii

It had a past once, a fragment of rock turning in the sea's mouth, but by lifting it from the beach, by putting it beyond change, there is no future it can go to; there is nothing left for it to become.

iii

If I did this, or broke it open in that way, I would be bringing the present back into its life, marking it with time, so that the light of that moment would fall on its minute inner chambers like the beam of a torch.

iv

The only death available to it is a violent death. Otherwise it will endure, surviving us all, being passed from house to house, unchanging, as present to those times as it is to our own.

A History of the Tongue

It lay idle on the beds of their mouths,
or came to life along a length of bone,
or on another's body;

and in time folded itself into a runnel
for a sound to pass through,
again and again;

and then fluttered for the sheer pleasure of it
in the wind of their breathing,
words rising from them like birds.

Silences

i

The silence in this room, in the room above it, in the sky
                                            above that ...
The whole house stands in it as it might in still water.
Occasionally, from the street, the sound of a passing car, or
                                            of birdsong,
or of people talking, their voices suddenly close by.
They reach only a short distance into the silence, these sounds.
They make a shallow groove in it that closes behind them
so that the silence is restored impeccably to itself.

ii

Is there a bedrock of silence, a point beyond which
it is unable to fall, an ultimate silence that keeps returning to
                                          this point
and is the same everywhere ? Does the silence in this room,
in the hall, in the garden, continually aspire to it, like the silence
in a place somewhere entirely different, in another country,
these two places aspiring to the same silence: the deep silence
of a wood, say, in England and a wood in America? You can
                                          imagine it
stretching across the world, a single thing that the particulars
                                        of sound,
of places, the particulars of our times, keep entering and leaving,
keep imparting something to – a character, a colour – and
                                        then vacating.

iii

The silence then and the silence now. The silence of this place
a hundred, two hundred years ago and the silence now.
A woman stands at a window in another century
and then turns into the silence behind her which is the silence
of her times, of other times, of this room even. What she did then,
what she might have spoken, the gestures she might have made –
is she the closer for this, as if her actions disturbed the same air,
the same element; as if the past, even history itself, move
                              differently there ?

iv

Two sounds, this evening, occurring in
the same silence; the sound of a bird
high up over the street; and the sound of a man
talking in his garden,
two sounds held together by the one silence.

v

She stands there in the darkness.
She is so much a part of the silence
that she might have been set in it, as in a wall.
She is as silent as the night, as the tree
that she looks at. Their silence
is her silence. The silence rests in them
as it rests in her. When she turns into
the room she carries it with her,
silence moving invisibly through silence.

The Moment

It was one of those close, windless mornings
when the smallest of sounds had the clarity of something
that is looked at through water: the sound of milk bottles
grazing a doorstep at the far end of the street;
two builders in conversation on the top plank
of a scaffolding, as if in the next room;
a woman's footsteps echoing between the houses.
And, while it lasted, there was a sense
of each of us occupying the same moment,
moving at the same pace, both separate and not separate.

Considering Fire

   i

It happened. There was a time, a place,
a man sharpening stones in a wood,
one spark and then a second
falling into the dry grass, the small flame

appearing suddenly beneath him,
trickling into the undergrowth, taking hold,
so different from the things in his hands
he didn't know where it came from.

   ii

I remember holding the magnifying glass
with its perfectly round, silver-rimmed face
and its long black handle

perfectly still over a little mound of dry leaves
until the impossible happened and a plume
of white smoke rose suddenly from its centre,

the three of us
sitting there at the end of break-time while something
quite beyond us came through the entrance we had made for it.

iii

If you saw it for the first time, a match striking against the side of a box, you would expect either nothing or, at the most, a small cloud of powder. Among the things you would least expect is what you get. You would think, *How can such a thing be born from such unlikely beginnings?*

iv

A room without fire, a struck match and then suddenly a flame, fully formed. Nothing and then something, as if the air was continually pregnant with flame.

v

At any one time there are countless candle flames alight in the world – in churches, in restaurants, in bedrooms ... What is the difference between one flame and another? There are small variations – a tapering flame, a bulbous flame, flames shaking in the wind – different shapes called up by the condition of the wick or the weather, but beyond that they are almost the same. Seen in this way they are not so much separate entities as drops from some vast reservoir of flame which is never seen. Reverse the film, unlight the candles, unstrike the matches, and the flames would be sucked back into the single source from which they came.

vi

It is easy to imagine a fraternity of flames, a universal brotherhood that keeps its silence, bides its time, observes us even.

vii

We arrange them around us like flowers. They are decorative, functional but also deadly. In their heart is a capacity for infinite pain. Run a finger through them and we feel its breath. It is strange that they should inhabit our various domestic interiors when they speak of a quite other world.

viii

And then I think, 'How obliging they are.' When you strike a match they assume precisely the right shape and when you carry this to a candle and deposit it there, they bloom gently from the wick, settling their pear-shaped bottoms into the small cup of wax beneath them. It could have been so different: a rocket of flame shooting suddenly to the ceiling, for instance.

ix

The gentle rattle of the candles when you dip your fingers into the candle box; the touch of the wax, as smooth as a crayon; five seconds of stillness while you tilt the wick of a new candle into the steady flame beside it before pressing it down into the holder, the peeled wax falling off the stem of it like pencil shavings. What is it we are doing? Creating something which survives our walking out into the street, the turning of our attention to other things?

x

Even in a hot, airless room they will suddenly quiver and bend, alert to currents of air that are beyond the register of our feeling.

xi

They never age. The wax melts around them, the wick burns to a stub but they are the same now as when they were first lit. Time appears to make no impression on them. They go, not of their own volition, but when the things they burn from – candles, firewood – diminish and dissolve beneath them.

xii

They are always almost there, on the edge of existence, waiting to be struck, or to fall through the side of a discarded bottle, pressing their faces against the glass of what is.

xiii

Think about them for long enough and they could begin to haunt you, creatures from another dimension that appear and disappear, running back and forth between our world and their world.

Visiting Birds

There is a cry they have
that sounds mournful
or melancholy, and a kind of chattering

that sounds mischievous.
It may be they are saying nothing
or saying something we have no words for,

calling out from a place
where language has never been,
where nothing of our own lives holds true.

Naming the Tree

i

There was the tree, something that was looked at,
and there was the word for it
sent among its branches, two different modes
encountering one another, the image
and the sound of it. There was a hovering
just then, a holding back. What had a word
to do with a tree? What place had it here?

ii

Something that was looked at,
that was familiar
only to the eye,
suggesting a sound for itself, another way

of existing in the world; an image
finding some kind of equivalence
in sound, the look of it –
its branches, its green leaves, their

movements in the wind – all clamouring to enter it.
An entering and a leaving, the tree resting only briefly
in the sound of itself; a passing through,
the word, the beginnings of a word, falling off it like a shell.

iii

What sound does an image speak?
What did the grass say to them, the water,
the trees ...? Was there a language
other than the language of their own sounds,
their own rustlings? Was there a character
to the tree, a figure, almost, within it
that spoke to them the perfect sound of itself?

X

A tree with its sound hanging from it and a world around it
where words hadn't ventured. In the distance
a mountain, a lake, regarded but no more –
white mountain, black lake –
so that the tree was loosened from its background,
was no longer of a piece with its surroundings
but a new creation, half a thing of the world, half of themselves.

The Making of Nests

   i

A kind of coming down to earth,
an entering into our way of things,
a sudden taste for the human, the domestic:
potato peelings, cotton wool, sweet wrappers,
all carried in their beaks to those saucers of air
they have started to make visible.

   ii

The trees are full of their desire,
a single thing that has crossed the fields
like a slow wind and entered the wood.

The flock of birds flapping around the branches
is the sight of it, what it looks like
once it has broken through the surface of itself.

The Mistake

Consider that the word we have for it
doesn't say what is true,

that it holds up its mirror
to an untruth, or a wrong way of seeing things,

and that the only way through this
is never to say it,

or to say it doubtfully,
hoping that its meaning

will gradually grow weaker,
hoping that in some way

we can start again, going back
to where the mistake was first made,

to that small patch of silence
in the middle of the language.

The Darkness

i

I know only a small part of them, the part I can see. I see them through the aperture of my sight which is the corridor they walk up and down in.

ii

At night they bang in and out of the cat-flap in quick succession. It makes me think of the pull that the night has on my daughter and her friends only for them it is the lights, the music. For the cats it is the darkness though they too come alive there, the same night running through them like electricity. At these moments I can follow them with my gaze to the end of the garden. Then they slip through a gap in the hedge which is that hole in my understanding.

iii

They are gone for the whole night. Sometimes, when I awake and hear them calling or screeching, I try and imagine what it is they are doing. It may be that that part of them which I know falls around them like clothes and what is revealed, what comes into its own, is desire, appetite. If I interrupted them, if I turned a light on them, I doubt they would know me. They would look up, straddled over their prey, and see no more than a stranger on the farthest horizon of their lives.

iv

In the morning they return, their coats smelling of cinders and garbage, the alcohol on their breath.

v

And ask to be fed. So I turn a fork around the inside of a tin while they step back into themselves (the tables and chairs resuming their familiar positions), their voices taking on again their plaintive, domestic note.

vi

After that they sleep for an hour or two and then drift around the house. I will come into a room and find them sitting on a table, looking out the window, or lying under a radiator in a position of sleep, though without sleeping, only their eyes moving, or washing themselves on the sofa. There is the action and them doing it and that is all.

vii

They don't live in time in the way that we do, climbing into it each morning, as you might into a boat, travelling the length of the day and then stepping out of it again in the evening, at night time. Rather, they lie at the very bottom of the river, like a stone, and time runs over them and around them. All they know is the colour of the water above their heads and the way it darkens towards evening.

viii

Sometimes, when I go away, they seem to forget that I exist, or perhaps fall into a despair I can never be party to so that, when I return and they see me standing at the far end of the garden in the pale suit I sometimes wear when I travel, the evening light falling, they run towards me ecstatically, as if I'd risen from the dead.

ix

The way their emotions have such a clear run of them; the way jealousy, for instance, can suddenly touch them with its massive voltage and throw them at one another without warning.

x

When they fall asleep, I imagine them drifting slowly to the bottom of themselves like sediment, coming to rest only a short distance from death, so that all that is left of them is the vacancy of their bodies and their hearts beating within them like something that has been left on.

Before

Somewhere
the meaning of a word,

before it becomes a word,
waits in the silence. It is as if

it has come as far as it can go
without being uttered. In a moment

it will change from one thing
into another, or its meaning

will tremble into a word,
into something barely familiar,

finding itself spoken,
finding itself understood.

The Bell

It hangs from a nail in the yard
and rings lightly in the wind.

There may be intricacies of the wind
that only the bell catches,
nuances that are lost
on the trees, on ourselves

as when a note by itself
sounds in the stillness.

The First Bird

When the first bird arrives and settles in a tree
you can imagine a thin coating of salt
on its feathers, something alien and bitter
that it brings to the woods, the fields. You can imagine
the look of the sea in its eyes as if

the immensity of it, its secrets
lay upon them like a film or like a preoccupation,
a continual dreaming. Is the tree it sits in
a watery tree? Does the sea
still roar in its branches? You watch it

take flight. It keeps diving through the air
as if to dry itself of the memory,
as if to recover what it has lost.
Gradually it will arrive.
Gradually the land will move into it.

The Naming of Days

i

A time perhaps when spring came towards them
and stood in the same place as winter,
or alighted on them from above, or carried them
in a great arc towards summer. Or when the sound of icicles
dripping in a wood took them backwards
into spring, towards the last time they heard it.
Or when the first sound of birdsong
called to them from the future and from the past.

ii

He went and she watched him go.
His absence was the forest emptying itself
of leaves and the nakedness of the branches.
Its length was the length of the winter nights
and the slow dawns. His coming back
was the light falling one morning and his stepping into it.

iii

He came, as he always did, to the lake.
How long was it since she died?
There was only his sorrow and the seasons
passing over it – winter, summer – seasons
beyond measure. The day of her death
would never come round again. It would move
like a ghost over the water and he would never see it.

iv

The movement of the light, its slow passing
across the face of a hill ... To find words for it,
to speak it, was to bring to it a movement
that wasn't its own. There was the light
and there were words changing into other words.

v

One sound and then the next
and then the sound after that,
a movement forward of the words themselves,
one word following another, one word
occurring later than another, and so time
taking on the pace, the direction of words,
time beginning to go somewhere.

vi

The word for winter. The way it held still
as the winds swept over it, the rains fell.
This was a sound that was not the weather.
It was a sound they carried within them
and kept safe there. There was a word now
for winter to come to, to settle in front of
and to move on from, a winter of their own.

vii

And there were days, there were words
in which longing, apprehension had to wait,
words they were caught in. On a certain day
he would return. See how her longing was drawn out
over those distances, how each word was endured.

The Wall

It ages in its own time.
Bricks split open
without warning, pockmarks
appear at random on the brickwork.

These are its days and nights.
How far do they carry it
into the future? What passages of time
do they speak for? A year might pass

in a day. Are there moments there
when time barely moves, when the sun
travels over it but its dark interior
is still and silent? Eventually

it will fall down, or be taken down,
a kind of falling into time, the sunlight
reaching into its darkness at a certain angle,
the days beginning to close over it.

Dead

A word had to be found for it
as a word had to be found
for *river* or for *tree*;
a certain sound had to carry its meaning.

It was named and the word came calling,
a thing of their own invention
which they closed their doors against,
which the language no longer welcomed.

Crossings

i

The choosing of the wood, the shaping of it
into a figure of eight, once and then a second time;
the boxing of it with side panels
steamed and then curved into the shape of a wave;
the incising of the circle.

Then the making of the neck: the finger board,
the mother-of-pearl inlays, the machine heads;
the attachment of strings.
Its standing there in the silence, in the dusty light.
It might be a sculpture, an elegant assemblage

of objects, of odds and ends. Its meaning
is unclear. It is as if its separate parts
had arrived there after dark,
had converged on some secret location.
All they do now is wait.

ii

A single stroke, the downward movement
of a hand, is what suddenly reveals it,
its meaning running to every part of it
like an electric current,
the whole inanimate object, the particular instrument

giving rise to the invisible, to a music
that is everywhere at once.
There is a distance between these two things,
between the instrument itself
and the sound of it, a minute interval,

where one medium breathes life
into another, where the visible, the tangible
assumes its equivalence in the air,
both familiar, a part of what it was,
a ghost of itself, and something quite other.

iii

You see it sometimes in the way an animal moves,
in the way its crossing of a field, or the lowering
of its head to drink, is that
and nothing more. And even a distraction –
the creaking of a branch in the wind

or the banging of a barn door – only turns it
from one clean action straight into another,
into the pure water of what it does.
A bird hovers over the corner of a field
and then moves to another corner, its desire

holding it in place like a wire. What is it
for it to drift off into a white sky,
to desire nothing, to be so empty, so vacant
that the bird is only what you see above you,
only its own shape floating away on the wind?

iv

Maybe a white page without any writing on it,
all the whiter because this is where we expect
to find words, is one equivalence of silence,
or as near to it as we can get, one medium
aspiring to the condition of another. Words collect there,

bearers of images and meanings, of sounds,
like something carried on their backs
or stitched right through them like minute skeletons.
In the background there is always the whiteness,
the distances between the words, the small spaces

within the letters themselves. They are the places
that are silent, or the silence that remains
when the words have been carved out of it.
They rest there as they might rest on thin air or on a sheet
of white light, something that keeps pouring through them.

Something Had Been Done

Lighting the candles in the square that evening,
making their way there
from lecture halls, from offices, turning into
the high-walled streets, uncertain what would happen,

one wick tilting into the wick beside it,
the rows of policemen watching dispassionately
from behind the barriers, was like discovering
what they felt. It was as if the coming to life

of each flame, its sheer being there, its
want of equivocation, was its own kind of courage,
or as if everything they had thought about and spoken
and doubted and gone back on had been drawn into

its simplicity, into a single word. The next morning,
looking at the photograph in the paper,
The Ocean of Light, their strength came back at them
like another view of itself. It would be harder now

to return to how they were, to undo
those journeys, to pretend they hadn't been there,
to put back the candles unlit. Something had been done
and they had seen themselves do it.

Days

   i

Our futures, everything
that eventually happens,
defers to their slow,

measured arrivals. Between them
falls the darkness
which is change

riding at anchor. Tell me
of the one boat
we never anticipate,

of how it always puts in
at the one beach
we are not waiting on.

   ii

After she had died
I was given her pocket diaries
with their gilt-edged pages
and crumpled silk markers
sprawling from the bottom of them
like tassels from a missal.

The days after her death,
the divided white pages,
were shockingly empty, as if
her footprints had stopped.
And then the day of her death,
that arbitrary date, waiting there for decades.

iii

It was Christmas Day.
Everyone agreed. The silence
in the streets; then two boys
on brand new bicycles
careering round the corner,
the chrome-work flashing in the sun;
then, in the afternoon, the Queen's Speech.

I marvel sometimes
at the way we know this, at the way
we move unerringly towards it,
migrating from one side of the year
to the other, alighting on
the same day at the same moment.

iv

She was taken out of the day
the way a figure
might be taken out of a picture.

There were certain rooms
she no longer occupied, certain stairs
that were the lighter for her absence.

And she wasn't there any more
for the day to enter her, for the light
to fall through her eyes, for a particular view

to accommodate her looking. It was as if
the world no longer saw itself through her gaze,
as if something irreplaceable had been closed up.

Rain

  i

It falls where it will,
watering fields

that have long since
vanished under cities,

its profligate downpours discovering only
gardens, window boxes, flower pots,

the remains of the earth,
the last places to comprehend it.

  ii

It was as if the whole town
had been ordered off the streets,
as if a command had been shouted.
People on their way to somewhere
ran suddenly into doorways.

Then slowly it grew heavier.
They stood there in the grey light,
in places they hadn't been before,
watching it come down.

This hadn't been asked for;
this came from a different world,
lowering itself into the day,
making room for itself,

so that everything that was happening –
journeys, conversations –
were swept into these places
and left there to wither:
everyone standing still,
everyone falling silent.

Not

  i

Not the day itself
so much as the place
where the day happens,
that emptiness that holds steady
while the day
passes through it;
that the light
leaves no mark on,
or the darkness;

a place out of time
where the years keep coming,
where history is still made.

  ii

There were people, long ago,
who came here, as we come here now,
stooping through the same doorway,

visitors to the same stillness
who are separated, not by the years or the centuries,
not by an exact rendering of time.

iii

As if the present they turned to
and the present that we ourselves turn to

was the same present,
a stillness in the room

that isn't finally of its time
or of its place.

iv

Perhaps this is where the notion of eternity
becomes real, where the idea of it
takes on the most ethereal of realities,
a minute movement into the world,
a reality still steeped in the thought
of itself and yet still a reality.

Late January

That moment in the year
when you can walk into a room
and notice for the first time
how the light has changed,

how the turning of the earth
and the pouring of sunlight through space,
those immense occurrences,
can brighten a wall.

One

In this primitive, magical state ... everything participated in everything else.
              Erich Neumann, *The Origins and History of Consciousness.*

There were no words then
to make one thing
into two. The trees
were still embedded

in the sky, and the rivers
and the river banks
and the birds that gathered there
ran into one another.

A whole people
would cry out as one,
or feel aggrieved as one,
and laughter could fill a wood.

Birds

i

They know the sky in the way that nothing else does: its distances, its currents, its changes of mood. They bring this knowledge back into our world and see everything through it: the rows of houses, the gardens, the cars parked tidily along the streets.

ii

There is a bird moving from tree to tree
that brings nothing to them except its own weight
and the sound of its calling, the presence
of the bird and the presence of the trees

joining one another, an undisturbed meeting,
a movement only of its small body
through the air, of its light interior, as if
one part of the day were being carried to the other.

iii

There are times when they do nothing, or appear to do nothing, floating slowly back and forth along the same length of air, or letting the wind catch one of their wings and have its way with them. It is as if their desires, their fears had slackened in them for a moment and their want of purpose, their simply being there, had come into its own.

iv

It sings the one song it is able to,
the perfect sound of itself –

of what it looks like, of how it moves,
of everything that belongs to it –

the rendering of these things
in sound, their existing in another medium.

v

And then, one evening, they find themselves in the fields, as if carried there by the wind. Nothing they can see or hear draws them across the water. And as slowly they begin to cross it, lifting into the air, the land receding behind them, something of their singularity, their separateness is lost to them, as if it had been taken up into the lengthening body of the flock, which then assumes its own identity, its own singularity. For weeks, for months they travel in this way, barely conscious any more, or conscious only as a single entity, passing through rain storms, through winds, the days coming and going like a light falling intermittently across their passage. And when they arrive, wheeling over the sudden greenery of fields and trees, they settle briefly and then disperse, emptying themselves from the body that carried them, falling again into their separateness, their differences.

Asides

For centuries they have walked into woods
and found branches sturdy enough
to bear their own weight

that small calculation
in the moment of their despair.

Monday

   i

It wasn't
and then it was. There was nothing,
only the days running into one another,
the sunlight moving without saying anything,
or speaking only very slowly its own language,

and there was the word, a little ornament
of sound that was suddenly ready,
like an unveiled object. It stood there
in the half-light, the window open,

the vast day outside being summoned
to turn, to contract itself
to its proportions, to pass through it.

   ii

Monday without a name,
or a day that was no more than itself,

that had nowhere to go
or to return to, nothing to come round to,

or was nothing more than the weather, a part of
winter and lost in it.

   iii

They had stood the day for so long in the word
that the day gradually became it,
as if, in the end, this was all it knew,
as if it was itself the first day of the week
and had a place there of its own.

iv

Those who woke to it for the first time,
who woke to the daylight, to the familiar brightness
beyond the window, and then to the sound of the word

entering their memories like a word
from another tongue. It was not a sound
that the day itself gave rise to, or that clung to it

the way the word for a river clung to a river
and spoke of nothing else, but the word
for an idea, the idea of the first day,

the pure thought of it being carried by the sound
like a strange vapour, something unearthly.

v

Those who were too old for it,
for whom the word, the idea,
was too difficult and so who lived

in the old time, in days of shadow
and changing skies, the word coming and going
in the speech around them, in the strange language
 of their children and their grandchildren.

vi

It is the word that keeps still
and the day that moves into it,

its particular weather blowing into its syllables
so that Monday is blustery,

the whole day buffeting its way
through the word

and then vacating it, Monday collapsing to the ground
and becoming a word again, a thing of the mind.

The Fact

Nobody knew what would happen.
By the evening it would be over
and they would know
but in the morning they knew nothing.

By the evening it would be beyond doubt
but until then there was doubt
and nothing else. The day would change
from being empty of this knowledge to being full of it.

And how it was spoken of, the words
that were used, that too would change.
In the morning there was so much talking,
so much speculation, but in the evening

a single fact would visit the language
and silence everything around it.

Singing the Blackbird

   i

It wasn't so much the blackbird
singing on its own in a tree

as the song in some way
singing the blackbird

as if the song had blown into it
from somewhere else

and all the blackbird had to do
was to open its beak.

   ii

How much of itself
rises from a branch
and flies into the distance

or is the whole flock,
a flock that is never seen,
even the whole species

so buried within it
that blackbirds everywhere
lift it into the air?

The Book

When the book was closed the words fell into the darkness,
the darkness of the closed book, pages without light,
less a book now than an object like any other,
a square object on a table, the light reflecting off its cover,
as if the look of it, the visible, was all it could claim for itself.

Inside it the words lost their meaning, or their meaning
froze in them or so faded into the letters
that the book became a book of letters only,
of shapes and markings, not even a book
but a container of some kind, a box. It rested in the light

as if resting in water, the light pressing on its cover,
on its spine but never entering it. Open it
even for a moment and the light would pour onto its pages
and its meaning would begin to stir. It was all readiness,
all waiting, something always on the edge of becoming
                                          something else.

When it was opened again, the light fell on the letters
and the words filled with meaning in a single movement.
It rose from them so brightly that the words were obscured by it,
one kind of light answering another, a book now
of pure meaning, almost invisible, almost weightless.

Oversteps Books Ltd

The Oversteps list includes books by the following poets:

David Grubb, Giles Goodland, Alex Smith, Will Daunt, Patricia Bishop, Christopher Cook, Jan Farquarson, Charles Hadfield, Mandy Pannett, Doris Hulme, James Cole, Helen Kitson, Bill Headdon, Avril Bruton, Marianne Larsen, Anne Lewis-Smith, Mary Maher, Genista Lewes, Miriam Darlington, Anne Born, Glen Phillips, Rebecca Gethin, W H Petty, Melanie Penycate, Andrew Nightingale, Caroline Carver, John Stuart, Ann Segrave, Rose Cook, Jenny Hope, Christopher North, Hilary Elfick, Jennie Osborne, Anne Stewart, Oz Hardwick, Angela Stoner, Terry Gifford, Michael Swan, Denise Bennett, Maggie Butt, Anthony Watts, Joan McGavin, Robert Stein, Graham High, Ross Cogan, Ann Kelley, A C Clarke, Diane Tang, Susan Taylor, R V Bailey, Alwyn Marriage, John Daniel, Simon Williams, Kathleen Kummer, Jean Atkin, Charles Bennett, Elisabeth Rowe, Marie Marshall, Ken Head, Robert Cole, Cora Greenhill and John Torrance.

For details of all these books, information about Oversteps and up-to-date news, please look at our website:

www.overstepsbooks.com